Cover Designed by Bruce J Carpenter

This is a work of reference material and stories as experienced by the author and recounted to the best of his personal (and highly opinionated) recollection. This is not intended to serve as an instruction manual as to the proper use or operation of firearms.
Any resemblance to actual persons, living or dead, events, or locales is entirely possible.

Bruce J Carpenter

Visit my website at: www.huntandfishmontana.com

Printed in the Untied States of America

First printing: May, 2021

ISBN: 9798507644094

"A good shot must necessarily be a good man since the essence of good marksmanship is self-control and self-control is the essential quality of a good man".

- Theodore Roosevelt -

I Had Arrived…

It was a sunny November afternoon in Montana and several of us were standing over the top of my very fine antelope buck, which was the fourth antelope buck taken so far that weekend in our party of five. My son Brad kneeled down to inspect the two entry holes in the animal as he asked me, *"How far did you say that shot was?"* In a tone of mild frustration, I said, *"It was 670 yards… but I can't believe he didn't go down with the first one and I had to make a follow up shot"*. Brad looked up at me and as he was pointing at the two entry wounds and exclaimed, *"Do you realize what you just did!?"* I pointed out once again my surprise that the buck had not expired with the first shot, to which my thirty-year-old son interrupted me with, *"Dad!... you just put two shots three inches apart in the kill zone on an animal at 670 yards... there's probably only three guys in the whole state who could do that!"* There was a long silence........... then my eyes actually welled up as I came to the realization that 20 years of work had all come together in that moment, allowing me to harvest yet another trophy animal at a considerably long distance, with incredible accuracy, under real-world conditions, on the plains of Eastern Montana.

I had become so accustomed to taking most of my animals with a single shot that the gravity of this particular situation had escaped me. Upon further investigation we realized that if I had only waited a few more seconds, he would have expired from the first shot, which had clipped the heart, causing massive blood loss… he simply refused to tip over, in spite of his mortal wound. It was a very emotional and proud moment for me, as I came to grips with what a truly epic journey had led me to this day.

The Inspiration…

My 20-year quest to become a proficient long-range marksman/hunter had started on the last day of Montana's hunting season 20 years earlier. On that day, with only 15 minutes of shooting light left, I found myself looking through my scope at the biggest mule deer buck I had ever seen in my life. In true trophy mule deer fashion, he was in a spot where he could see anything coming from a mile in any direction, and he was still somewhere between 800 and 1000 yards even after I belly-crawled for 10 minutes in an attempt to close the gap before dark. I had no rangefinder, no elevation adjustment on my scope, and no idea how much bullet drop there would be at any distance past 350 yards... I was simply uneducated in these matters. So, I lobbed two bullets in that deer's direction, and it was only after the second shot, that he jumped and took off running when the bullet fell short and sprayed him with dirt. He, and the 10 mature does he was with, were gone… but I was left with the inspiration to never let that happen again.

…20 years later, I was shooting the exact same rifle, with my own precision hand loads, and the same scope with an elevation knob now installed. I had just harvested the biggest and most beautiful antelope buck of my lifetime at what many hunters would consider an impossible shot distance at best. It was at this moment that I realized how far I had actually come from that day when I watched a 38" wide mule deer buck trot over a hill a mile away, never to be seen again.

My 2020 Montana Boone and Crocket Moose… (it was a 30-year wait applying for this tag).

The Journey…

I grew up in a family where we harvested meat out of necessity and antlers were seldom considered in the taking of any animal. My first 10 big game animals were killed at less than 250 yards and we simply didn't think about shooting much farther than that. Back then, if an animal was more than 300 yards away, we either let it go or worked on sneaking closer. As a youth, I remember those occasionally frustrating trips with my father, watching the big bucks simply bound away because they were more than 300 yards. In my mind, I knew that it was possible for a bullet to go much farther than that and kill an animal cleanly… except trophy hunting was not our purpose at that time, we were primarily there for the meat and not the headgear.

It was only after starting my own life as an adult that I began to realize that I was somewhat of a natural with a rifle in my hands. The geometry and math of it all simply clicked with me. I would run scenarios of distance and speeds in my head as mental exercises. I remember driving down the road on one antelope trip thinking to myself…

> *"My bullet travels roughly 3000' per second out of the muzzle, which is a 1000 yards per second so roughly 1/10 of a second per 100 yards... An antelope running flat out moves at about 45 miles per hour, times 5280 feet (one mile), divided by 60 minutes, divided by 60 seconds, equals roughly 66 feet per second at a dead run... which calculates out to 6.6 feet of travel for every 10th of a second. Then I factor in the 1/10 of a second travel time for every 100 yards for my bullet... So, a 200 yard shot would require me to lead an antelope at a dead run by just a smidge over 13 feet.... That would be a really tough shot to judge!... Probably best to avoid the running shots altogether".*

Then I remembered the story of the time that a string of antelope ran past one of my father's hunting buddies, who lined up on the lead buck and was shocked when the third doe back crumpled into a pile when the shot went off. It made me chuckle, then it made me realize what an incredibly difficult, and therefore irresponsible, shot that was.

These mental exercises were a fascinating train of thought for me, with the hundreds of different scenarios, wind factors, speed and angle variables, etc. It all started to come together in my mind in a very clear picture. My first thought was that taking shots at moving animals would be extremely difficult to calculate, therefore, targets that were standing still would be much preferred. Typically, these targets were the ones that were unaware of my presence, because I was either very sneaky, or very far away. The second thought was that I needed to educate and equip myself with the proper tools and information, so I could effectively and consistently achieve very long shots at those stationary animals. These thoughts would ultimately allow me to put more trophies on the wall, and doing so with quality shot placement.

It was then that I started doing serious research, and I began asking a lot of questions of a lot of people who all had different perspectives on shooting. This led me to develop my own practical list of important factors required to become an effective long-range hunter… not just a *"marksman"* shooting paper targets at the range, but a responsible, ethical, practical, and effective *"hunter"*. There are so many factors in being an accurate shooter, especially in real-world conditions, so I composed this list with the idea that I could share much of my 20 years of learning and practical experience with others.

While there is no substitute for learning good spotting, stalking, and belly-crawling skills, there will always be that hunt where you simply cannot get to a place where you have a *"relatively close"* shot, typically due to time constraints or uncooperative terrain. Remember that this information is about ***"practical"* long-range shooting for hunters**, and that by *"long-range"* I mean 600 to 1,000 yards… Always keeping in mind that the intention is to harvest each animal *cleanly, with a single shot.*

There will no doubt be many critics of my perspectives and of some of the technical aspects I employ in my own shooting and hunting techniques. Many of these critics might well be able to out-shoot me at the range off a bench, or from a mat laid out on the flat ground. However, most of them would not do well with an *"Eye-Poppin-Wall-Hanger"* in their scope at dusk, a 20-mph cross wind, laying in 6" of snow, and 800 yards to the target after just having hiked 5 miles, (without lunch). Everyone is entitled to their opinion, mine simply results in the ability to put more trophy animals on the wall than most of the so-called *"experts"*. This material is NOT preparation for competition shooting of a highly repetitive nature under controlled conditions. **The purpose here is to simply give you much of the practical and proven information you need to develop the skill set to put a bullet through the vitals of an animal at long distance in real-world conditions.**

The List….

1. **Natural ability and comfort with a rifle:** There is simply no substitute for that level of comfort and confidence that comes naturally while holding a firearm. If you don't already have it, you can still develop this with training, repetition, field experience, and a wealth of knowledge that will give you great confidence when the time comes to take that long shot.

2. **Staying calm, maintaining focus, and being patient:** *"Buck Fever"* is the single biggest cause of missed shots and wounded or lost game. The psychological aspects of getting a bullet on target can easily outweigh all of the technical, equipment, or environmental issues of any shot, and must be the first hurdle to overcome on the long road to becoming an effective marksman/hunter.

Actual cell-phone photo through my scope (2020).

A dozen times, I have witnessed a hunter jack out the already chambered live round onto the ground in their state of overwhelming excitement. This was often accompanied by the bolt not being brought back far enough to catch the rear of the next round in the magazine, and then being thrust forward pushing nothing but air. Few things are more frustrating than the **CLICK-JERK… "DAMMIT!"**

There is no one-size-fits-all answer to overcoming the heart-pounding, heavy-breathing, didn't-chamber-a-round, adrenaline-driven sickness that is *"Buck Fever"*. I do know that you MUST find a relative calmness that only comes from spending a lot of time out in the field with the animals that you will eventually put in your freezer. One thing that I can strongly recommend is making a conscious decision to NOT squeeze the trigger on the first 5 or 10 animals you put your scope on each season. Leave the safety on, or better yet, don't chamber a round when you look at the first ones, simply practice observing and setting up for the shot while you go through your mental checklist… RELAX… and take some time to actually watch the animals in the scope and learn their behaviors, even if it is only for a few seconds. Simple observation will naturally bring a calm to you that will allow you to focus on the necessary steps to a clean kill. Staying calm and a well placed shot builds confidence, which in turn, brings a greater sense of calm during those important moments. The calm and the confidence build upon each other as your skill level and understanding increase.

I spotted the deer in the above photo at 1000-plus yards, snuck to a position on a knoll and prepared for an 800 yard shot. I had opportunities for clean shots at 800 yards, 600 yards, and 500 yards as the buck slowly meandered his way down the mountain… I shot him at 60 yards with only 3 minutes of shooting light remaining, without moving from that spot! My two great advantages were that he never knew I was there, and PATIENCE. As he slowly came closer, I kept adjusting the focus/distance knob on the scope, reduced the magnification to allow a better sight picture, ranged him regularly and adjusted the elevation on the scope to match the yardage. Those are a lot of things to keep track of and could only be done effectively by someone who is remaining calm. The best part was that I had saved myself having to drag the animal the extra 800 yards back to the vehicle.

Calm helps you evaluate the situation and make good choices and good shots. So… did you see the small buck in the previous photo of the two bull elk in my scope? Did you see the tops of the antlers of the third bull walking in from the right in a depression behind those bulls? Often times, we miss very important things because the excitement makes us focus so intently on one particular thing. Remember that the single greatest advantage to long-range hunting/shooting is that the animals seldom know that you are there. This gives you so much more time to look around, observe, and make better choices… there simply isn't any need to rush things most of the time.

3. **Practice shooting until you're comfortable:** This does not mean buy 500 rounds of ammo and shoot them all to simply get yourself comfortable with the recoil… That's just *"pulling a trigger"*... *"Shooting"*, on the other hand, is the culmination of the many different disciplines and behaviors that allow a person to put a bullet very accurately on a target at distance. Practice with multiple firearms and develop techniques that work for you with all rifles, and don't put hundreds of rounds through the gun you plan on being your *number one long distance rifle*… rifle barrels do wear out (like everything else) and can become less accurate after many rounds are fired.

   Practice taking shots in many different real-world situations with the SAFETY ON. There really isn't any need to actually send a bullet down range every time you pull the trigger once the ammunition and rifle are dialed in. Lay down in the grass or on uneven terrain and practice every aspect of holding the rifle steady while you look through the scope at a long-distance target, and make sure that you are able to keep the crosshair steady through the entire process. Shooting from a bench is ideal for rifle tuning and sight adjustment, though it won't give you the necessary knowledge acquired from laying in the dirt like you will while out hunting. Try using cartridge simulators also so you can actually experience the trigger feel without the distraction of the explosion.

4. **Take care of your rifle:** We have all been hunting with the guy who throws his gun in the truck and bangs his scope on the console, or lays it on the back seat with a shotgun and a lunch cooler bouncing down 40 miles of gravel roads… Yikes! Keep your rifle in a padded hard case (not a soft case) until you need to have it ready, and do everything possible to keep the vibrations and impacts to a minimum. Remember, this is all about *"long-range shooting"* and it takes a finely tuned, precision instrument to shoot a 4 inch group at 600 yards. Machinists keep their calipers in padded hard cases… professional photographers don't just throw their cameras on the seat while driving around… many of us even have padded pouches for our sunglasses… So why wouldn't you protect your rifle as best you can?

   It's always a good idea to keep a clean and well lubricated firearm, but for goodness sakes, **don't over-clean your barrel**! A couple of oiled patches is more than enough to clean the residue left by a dozen rounds, and one stroke with a bore brush for every 40-50 shots is plenty. There seems to be a school of thought out there that vigorous bore cleaning using chemicals, brushes, and even electrical current is necessary. Too many people have simply *"scrubbed the accuracy right out of their guns"* through excessive bore cleaning.

   If you are having problems with carbon or copper fouling, the real problem is with the ammunition and the loading. Another damaging school of thought is that *"faster bullets are better"* and this leads some people to increase powder loads and decrease bullet weight to increase bullet speed. Doing this causes fouling and wear in the bore and will decrease accuracy in most cases and certainly decrease the life of the barrel in the long-term. You wouldn't drive your new truck around with the throttle to the floor… so why would you do that to your rifle? Take care of the one thing that is going to help you put more trophy antlers on the wall.

   Don't forget to take care of your rangefinders, binoculars, spotting scopes, and your ammunition as well. Why some people carry their sunglasses in a padded case and yet put extra ammo for their rifle in a fully exposed elastic bullet holder on the side of their gun or in their open ammo belt is beyond me. Those are fine if you are hunting heavy brush with open sights on a 30-30, not if you have a finely tuned rifle and precision loaded ammo that you now scrape on trees, rocks, grass, car doors, and allow to get wet and dirty before you put those cartridges into your precision rifle… YIKES! One small scratch in a bullet can cause a huge deviation in point of impact at longer ranges. Keep your optics in padded holders and your ammo clean, dry, and undamaged.

5. **An accurate rifle barrel is essential:** Some rifle barrels are extremely accurate and consistent, and some will never give you a good grouping no matter how much time or money you put into the weapon or the ammunition. NO! You do not have to spend a fortune on a high-end rifle in order to have a tack driver.... Today, I still hunt with the same Remington rifle that I ordered at the gun counter at Walmart 20 years ago and I have done no modifications to the gun itself… it was an absolute tack driver right out of the box, and still is. I installed a Leupold scope with beefy rings on a solid, one-piece 20 m.o.a. scope base. I typically shoot less than 15 rounds a year through it and it only sees a bore brush once every 2 years.

One of the first things I learned from talking to hundreds of people about the accuracy of their rifles was the luck of the draw in getting an extremely accurate rifle barrel. Many individuals had purchased multiple-thousand-$ rifles and spent months and hundreds of rounds with dozens of load variations only to sell the guns or install new barrels after never being able to achieve a good sub-m.o.a. group. If you buy a new rifle with a well mounted, quality optic and a box of high-quality target ammunition, you will know within the first six shots off a solid bench whether or not you have a sub-m.o.a. barrel… if it's not, don't waste *too much* time trying to find out why it's not accurate. Check the obvious things of course, like trying different ammo, loose scope mounts, and always let someone else shoot the rifle to eliminate the possibility that it's simply just you. You may spend a lot of money and cause yourself a lot of frustration and ultimately end up getting a different firearm or a different barrel put on the rifle. Don't get caught up in justifying the price you paid for the weapon, if it's a custom rifle from a reputable manufacturer, make arrangements to send it back to them for replacement or a barrel swap. Remember that only about half of *"marksmanship"* is due to the equipment, and bad equipment can be replaced easily.

Eastern Montana 2007 – 287 yards – Two minutes of legal shooting light left.

6. **Whatever technique works for you:** The single biggest factor in accuracy is your ability to maintain rifle stability. We can all understand how clamping a rifle into a massive vice, and having minimal human contact with the weapon creates the most accurate shots... Unfortunately, it's not very practical to expect that kind of stability in real-world situations, so you've got to figure out *what works best for you*, then do that at the range and in the field. A very popular topic of conversation with sportsmen and/or marksmen regarding accuracy is all about technique. I have been schooled on no less than 17 different breathing techniques, 29 different ways to hold a rifle, 24 body positions, leg positions, one-eye, two-eyes, how to hold your mouth, what to eat 2 weeks prior to the start of hunting season, and those that swear that they must have a cup of coffee to calm their nerves before shooting. You know what?.... They were ALL correct! Well how can that be you say? Because I realized after a while that these people were not trying to tell me what I should be doing, they were all simply telling me what worked for them.

   In the mix of all of this, there were still a handful of wannabe sharp-shooters that were frustrated and stuck on some pearls of wisdom that some *"expert"* had them believing was *"the only technique that will work"* so they refused to venture into the unknown and try new things. Some of these people could never put a sub-m.o.a. group on a target because they simply refused to try something different. Don't let stubborn pride or fear be the reason that you remain an average shooter. Try different things, be open to new techniques... worst case scenario, you throw a few bullets down range that don't hit the target, and you learn some things that maybe didn't work for you. You will only really ever know what works for you after you consistently start putting 3 shots in a nickel size group at 100 yards.

7. **You absolutely MUST get over the fear of recoil:** I have hunted with people who refused to shoot prone because they were terrified of their own rifle's recoil. If you can't get past the fear, you may as well resign yourself to taking 100 yard shots for the rest of your life. If you fear the shot, you will unconsciously hold the gun tightly, tremble, close your eyes, and jerk the trigger. Once you logically conclude that ***you are NOT going to be injured or die*** when the gun goes off, and that you can take a little thump on the shoulder, then you will be able to focus on all of the other things necessary so you can put the bullet where you want it.

   The best way to know if you are afraid of the recoil is to go to the range and fire some rounds at a target right before dark. If you don't see the muzzle flash in the scope, it's because your eye was closed!... your scope eye should NEVER be closed when the gun goes off. If you are squeezing the trigger properly, you will be somewhat surprised every time when the gun goes off, and if your eye is open you will get a temporary *"visual imprint"* of exactly where the crosshair was on the target at the millisecond of detonation. With this visual imprint, 95% of the time, you will know exactly where the bullet is going to land before your gun even settles back onto the target. Keeping your eye open can be difficult to overcome, though you will be so pleased with the increase in your accuracy that you will actually start looking forward to seeing the next *"visual imprint"* from each shot. More importantly, you will know when you have made a good shot and not go into panic mode trying to get off a second shot because you will already know where the crosshair was when the gun went off and that you have a good hit.

Make a plan with every first shot to keep your eye open, to quickly reacquire the target in the scope after the gun settles, and to *evaluate what is happening* with the animal **before** becoming concerned with getting another round in the chamber. I quite often witness (through the scope) the impact of the bullet on very long shots, and I will typically watch the animal through the scope for 3-5 seconds after the first shot before determining whether or not I should be chambering another round. When you realize that there are a dozen more important aspects of taking a shot than getting a thump on the shoulder, you will understand that putting all your focus on recoil means that you are *not* focusing on the things that are going to get the bullet where you want it.

My 2020 Mountain Whitetail, 80 yards...
Always be ready for a close shot - Keep your scope turned down, just in case.

8. **Consistent and motionless trigger pull:** A friend was getting 2-inch groups on the bullseye at 100 yards at the range one day when I offered to shoot his rifle to see if we could figure out how to tighten up his groups. So, I took his gun and put a 4-shot, ¾" group on a new target… that group was 2" left and 5" high! We were both amazed at the relatively consistent trigger pull he had down and to the right. This simply goes to show that all the setup in the world won't give you a clean shot if the gun moves during the trigger pull.

   This brings me to the terms "trigger pull" or *"trigger squeeze"* … I like to replace that term with ***"trigger pinch"***. Sometimes perspective is everything and simply viewing trigger activation from a different perspective can make a huge difference in shot consistency. The third law of physics states that *"for every action there is an equal and opposite reaction."* So, imagine your rifle is sitting on a table with the bipod legs holding it upright, then imagine what happens to the rifle when you put just your finger on the trigger and push it backwards… the entire rifle wants to move. Next, picture your trigger hand wrapped around the rifle and the palm of your hand pushing forward on the stock while your finger pulls back on the trigger… since your palm is primarily on the side of the stock, the gun may experience a tilting or twisting motion as you squeeze. Now imagine your trigger hand wrapped around the gun only lightly brushing the stock with just enough force to hold the crosshair vertical while your thumb is placed where the rear of the action meets the stock right behind the bolt and your finger is on the trigger… then you slowly *"pinch"* the trigger between only your thumb and finger in a straight line through the centerline of the action, as though you are gently squeezing an egg with exactly the same amount of pressure on both sides with only your thumb and finger, thus generating two equal and opposite forces that cancel each other out.

   There is a myth floating around that *"triggers must be pulled straight backward"*, and *that simply is NOT true*. Nearly all rifle triggers are on a pivot point that allows you to pull back and slightly up while *"pinching"* forward and slightly down with your thumb. The thumb/finger *"pinch"* allows for no force to be applied in any other direction than between the two points, thus virtually eliminating movement of the rifle caused by trigger activation.

9. **Refine and practice rifle stability techniques:** If you want to be a serious long-range shooter, you simply must avoid certain things and ultimately **keep the crosshair motionless as the gun fires… no matter what!** Shooting from a prone position with a bipod is by far the most stable position possible. Don't even consider the idea of NOT having a bipod mounted to your rifle if you want to be shooting at game in open country more than 500 yards. If you cannot shoot prone,

then you will be limiting yourself to 500 yards at best from a seated position with a taller bipod, or 300 yards standing with quality shooting sticks.

As you walk/hike, you should always be looking for the next spot for a good setup free of obstacles … having these patches of open ground already picked out may save valuable time if you need to make a quick prone shot. Don't walk through waist-high brush expecting to be able to make a 700 yard shot… because you won't have a place to rest your gun. Shooting over the hood of a vehicle (aside from the obvious legalities and safety issues) is only a reasonable idea if the vehicle is turned off, nobody else (including the dog) is inside the cab, and the wind isn't blowing. Likewise, setting your gun on a sagebrush in the wind, a fluffy folded jacket, over your buddy's shoulder, or on a small branch, are all unstable rest setups for 500-plus yard shots… hard ground, rocks, and logs work well. **Always choose a solid rest**!

10. **Always keep the crosshair vertical:** Because the rifle is launching the bullet in a somewhat vertical trajectory at longer ranges, if the gun is tilted slightly the bullet is then cast to the left or right. A mere one degree angle of tilt in the rifle/scope can cause a bullet to impact 24" to one side at 600 yards, depending on the ballistics of a particular cartridge. A bipod with a tilting head is a must for both stability and keeping the crosshair in a true vertical orientation on uneven ground. Installing optics with built-in bubble levels or aftermarket bubbles is a good option if you have difficulty judging a true vertical crosshair. Remember though, every gadget or additional process you add can also be one more time-wasting distraction that may create a lost shot opportunity, so learn to rely on your own ability to *"see"* the whole sight picture and less on gadgets.

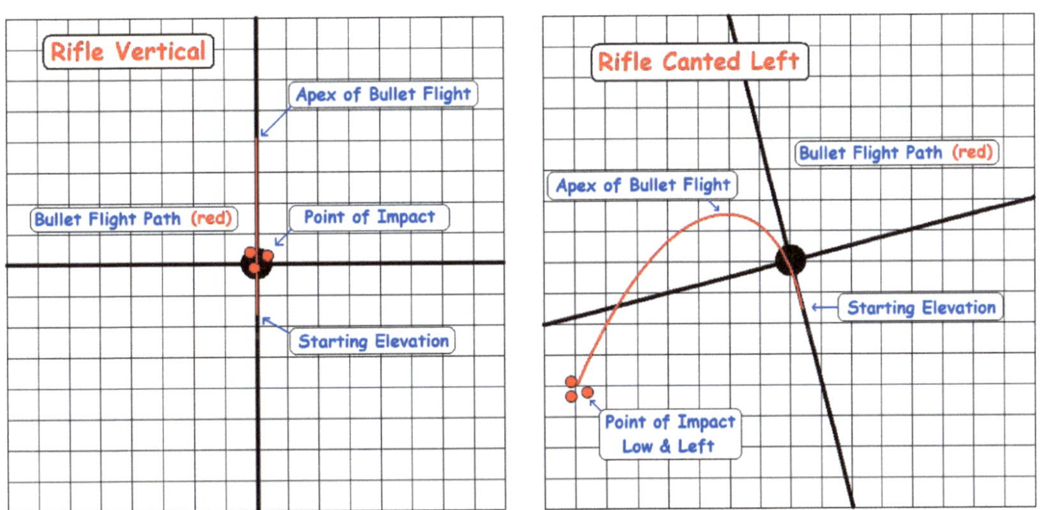

These diagrams show what will happen with a bullet's trajectory if the scope is not held perfectly vertical as the bullet leaves the rifle.

11. Limit transference of body motion into the rifle: The human body is constantly in motion with twitching muscles, breathing and especially the beating heart and pulsing blood flow. All these motions can transfer through your body very easily and into a weapon that needs to be held absolutely still. If you have any doubts that your pulse is a factor, simply sit upright in a chair with one leg crossed over the other, then sit as still as you can and watch the floating foot as it moves in sync with your heartbeat… now imagine your heart pounding with excitement as you look through your scope at the biggest buck you've ever seen, and how that pounding will cause your torso and limbs to move.

During any shot, the body never stops moving, so less contact with the rifle means less motion in the crosshairs. Ideally, we would like to be able to shoot without touching the rifle at all… that simply isn't very practical however. I have heard dozens of people giving instruction to new shooters, and one of the first things they say is *"pull the rifle tight into your shoulder"*… BAD IDEA! Doing this is a real accuracy killer, and it is typically practiced by those who are *afraid of the recoil* (another reason to conquer your fear of recoil).

Shooting prone with a bipod and employing the *"trigger pinch"* method from **#8** works very well with some additional key techniques. Setting up for those particularly long shots is especially critical. Always position yourself so the bullet will not hit *anything* when you take the shot. Remember that the sightline of the scope is well above the bullet path. I have seen shooters cut a trench through the dirt in front of them with the bullet, even though they had a clear sight picture of their target. Even a single blade of grass can deflect a bullet several feet at the target.

238 yard neck shot (dropped in his tracks) 2016

Take a moment to adjust the bipod height for better stability and angle when necessary as you set up for a long shot. With *any* bipod, you should always use the non-trigger hand to support the butt of the rifle and let the bipod support the front end when shooting prone. Your trigger hand is only there to apply slight pressure on the stock to keep the crosshair vertical and to perform the *"trigger pinch"*. **The trigger hand IS NOT there to hold the back of the gun up, and neither is the shoulder!** With the bipod at the right height, you can easily make a thumb-up fist with the non-trigger hand and put it under the butt end of the stock so that neither your shoulder nor your trigger hand has any responsibility in setting the elevation of the rifle, nor will they cause any unnecessary movement of the rifle. Squeezing or releasing your fist will allow you to raise or lower the butt of the stock very smoothly. Occasionally, you may have to grab a rock, stick, or glove to put under your fist if it is not quite tall enough, or simply adjust the bipod down some… DON'T use the trigger hand to pull the butt of the rifle up!

Again… *NEVER* pull the rifle tight against you shoulder when using a bipod! You should just feel the butt end of the stock touching the fabric of your jacket without it putting any amount of pressure against the shoulder. *"Pulling"* the rifle into your shoulder requires the trigger hand to do so, and that hand already has the most important job, the *"trigger pinch"*. Even with a taller bipod in a seated position, the non-trigger hand should be holding the butt of the rifle up, not the shoulder. The shoulder is attached the heaving, pulsing torso where most of the accuracy-killing body movement comes from. About ½" of actual space between the butt stock and the shoulder can greatly increase accuracy, which is not nearly enough to allow the scope to contact your face upon recoil.

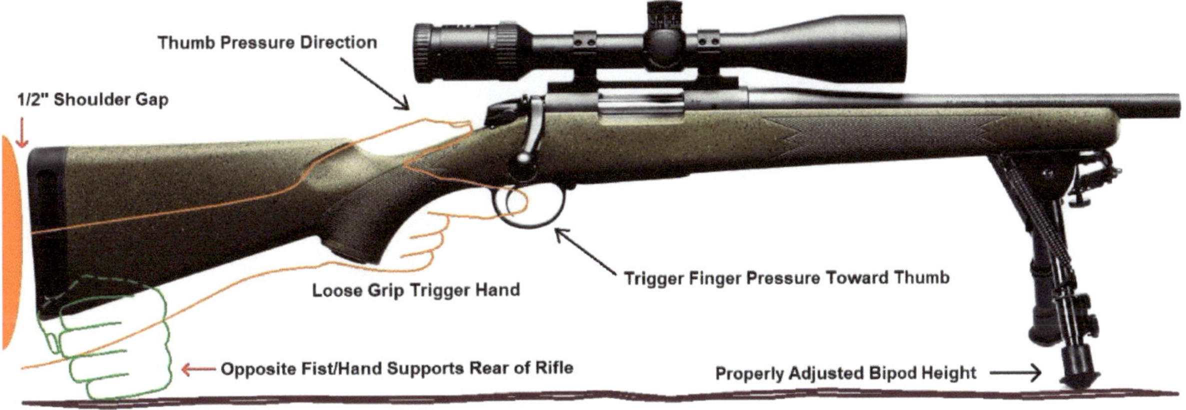

The **bipod and fist method,** along with the **trigger pinch** offers a very solid 3-point rest that will minimize the transference of body motion into the rifle.

12. **Accurate scope mounting is crucial:** Because of the vertical crosshair sensitivity, it is extremely important that the scope is mounted perfectly vertical on the rifle. There are bubble level aids that can help when mounting a scope, however, in my experience, simply lining up the bottom of the vertical crosshair with the centerline of the back of the bolt works well. Do this while looking through the scope from the butt of the rifle, and while centering the image in the glass. If you are using bubble levels and the crosshair doesn't seem to be vertical when the action and the scope boss/cap both level, there may be an internal alignment issue. I have seen many new scopes with caps or bosses that were NOT perpendicular to the crosshair inside the tube and caused the crosshair to move up and down at an angle when adjusted. If your new scope doesn't look right, send it back!... never assume that the price tag or brand name will automatically ensure the alignment of the crosshairs in the tube.

This scope is incorrectly mounted...

The crosshair does NOT line up with the centerline of the action/bolt (indicated by the white line).

Before fully tightening the scope, practice acquiring a full sight picture in all shooting positions. The *"full sight picture"* is when you see a clean, crisp circle and reticle with no foggy or faded edges. Position the scope in the rings where your eye naturally sits when you hold the rifle. You shouldn't have to stretch your neck or move your head back to see a full sight picture. You may need to loosen and move the scope several times before you find that *"just right"* location in the rings.

Notice the crisp image edges that are not fuzzy or faded...
this is how you know that your eye is in the perfect location relative to the scope.

Remember to use an alternating and progressive tightening sequence on the scope mounting hardware to prevent the scope from being rotated or misaligned as the rings clamp down on the scope tube. Use an adjustable torque driver set at the proper value for your hardware whenever possible. If you are having someone else mount your scope, find a person who comes highly recommended as an individual with long-range shooting experience... Quite often this person will not be found at the same place that you purchase your firearm or optics. Most sporting goods stores are full of *"salesmen"* who may or may not actually know what they are doing. After having multiple optics mounted incorrectly and fastener heads stripped by others, I personally refuse to let anyone else mount my optics.

13. **Some unpopular truths:** The psychosomatic effects of doing certain *"improvements"* to a rifle quite often results in a shooter having improved accuracy, though often the reality is that there was *no actual change* to the capabilities of the rifle, only improvements to the attitude of the shooter. This *placebo effect* is very real with some shooters, and falls into the *"do whatever works"* category… Ultimately, **Anything that makes a shooter feel better about their rifle or themselves is a positive thing.**

Many commonly mistaken beliefs are born when someone does multiple improvements to their rifle and their accuracy at the range improves. The truth may be that only one of the changes actually made the difference… or perhaps none of the changes made a difference, and what really changed was the shooter's confidence in their own weapon. Then they tell everyone that *"bedding the action"* or *"the latest scope rings"* were the real cure. Then Bob tells Joe, who tells Dean, who tells Julie, who tells Fred… and before long they all have new scope rings, or a glass bedded action that they didn't really need… and are wishing they had more beer money instead. However, if these *"improvements"* make them each have more confidence and/or improved accuracy, then who am I to say it wasn't necessary.

Sometimes, these simple misguided trends, that lead others to believe that the same improvements will *"solve"* their own accuracy issues, may instead lead them to a great deal of frustration when accuracy does not improve. This could result in a compounding lack of confidence in themselves and their rifle that may result in the need to abandon a weapon altogether and replace it with something completely different. We have all had *"bad experiences"* that lead to fundamental beliefs that simply aren't true… and yet we still believe them to be. I know people who refuse to shoot an antelope with a .30 caliber rifle because they are absolutely certain that it will *"blow the animal into pieces!"* Others who will never own a .270 Win. because they are convinced that *"it is a very inaccurate cartridge"*. My personal favorite is those who have no faith in any rifle that is not glass bedded, to the point where they will take a brand-new rifle to the gunsmith for bedding before ever even firing a single shot?!?!

There is often little basis for many of these common, emotionally driven beliefs about some gun issues. I do know for certain that if you question your rifle right out of the box, you will struggle with accuracy at the range indefinitely and may never be able to work on your own contributing factors to the problem because you will always be blaming the rifle. Remember that half of all accuracy issues are due to the shooter, and you MUST be willing to assume that you are the problem at times.

Gun stocks have been falsely blamed on far too many occasions for accuracy issues with rifles. The truth about *most* hunting rifles with a free-floated barrel is that the barrel, action, trigger, scope, rings, and scope base are a complete unit that is merely being supported by the stock. Many people don't realize that you can take the stock off of a gun and clamp the action, (with scope and barrel still attached), in a padded vise, and it will be every bit as accurate when fired. The stock exists to position these components in a manner in which the user can hold them steady for a quality shot, and to direct the recoil into the shoulder. Stocks also provide a forward handhold, and a mounting location for a bipod and sling.

This picture shows that the scope, action, trigger, and barrel assembly is a totally self-contained unit. The relationship of these components (and therefore the accuracy) is unaffected by the attachment of the stock (unless it touches the barrel or warps the action when mounted).

Many people don't understand that a free-floated barrel on a rifle only touches the gun where it threads into the action… you can slide a piece of paper all the way down to the action between the barrel and the stock. If there is contact anywhere between the two, it will need to be addressed because the barrel may be pushed slightly out of alignment when the temperature or humidity change. If contact with the stock causes the tip of the barrel to move only 8 one-thousandths of an inch (0.008"), this could cause a 10" deviation in shot placement at 800 yards.

A properly free-floated barrel does NOT touch the stock… Only the action.

First-shot deviation of black colored rifle barrels on very cold, yet sunny days can easily be as much as 10" at longer ranges as the sun warms one side of a cold rifle barrel causing it to warp ever so slightly. Thin wall, lightweight, and flat black barrels are even more susceptible to this problem. Stainless steel and light-colored, coated barrels reflect much of the sun's heat. A quickly removeable sock will also minimize this seldom-considered effect on accuracy.

I have heard a hundred stories about triggers, and which one is the best… it all boils down to personal preference and whatever makes you *"feel good"*. My twenty-year-old Remington has a factory trigger with a slight catch in it. I know my trigger and I can still put three in a row on a business card at 300 yards. There isn't any right or wrong with trigger selection, right up to the point where the gun is going off before you want it to because of an overly sensitive trigger. I don't ever suggest putting a very light trigger in any *hunting* rifle because the circumstances in the field vary so much. You may occasionally have to shoot with a glove on, and you will need to feel the trigger through the glove fabric. This is where you might say, *"I'll just take my glove off"*. I can tell you of 50 different instances where I laid on the ground, ready to take a shot for more than twenty minutes, in below-freezing temperatures, and was very glad I still had my gloves on. I remember several occasions, watching animals running away as a hunter turned around and said to me, *"I couldn't feel the trigger because my fingers froze… I had my glove off the whole time… the shot went off before I was ready!"* So…. NO, taking your glove off isn't always a good solution to having a desire for a super-sensitive trigger.

The need for glass bedding actions has been very much overly exaggerated as an *"accuracy killer"* based on the idea that when the action moves slightly in the stock it is *"knocked out of zero"*....This is ***absolutely false,*** because the relationship of the barrel and scope to the action doesn't change, even if the action moves. If the action is tightly seated and the barrel is free-floating while you activate the trigger, then wherever the crosshairs are when the gun fires is what will determine bullet placement. The stock itself does NOT determine the aiming point. On occasion, the stock may be applying enough force to warp the action a couple of thousandths of an inch, which can affect accuracy. In reality, action warping is **very rare,** and is usually caused by over-torquing of the stock mounting hardware.

Glass bedding is occasionally necessary to correct poor stock fit, or interference with the barrel, though the hype over bedding actions is ten times more exaggerated that the actual problem. It is often one the first of many attempts by gun owners to correct accuracy issues that are actually being caused by the barrel, ammo, optics, or human problems. If you can acquire a target quickly and easily in the scope, and the action is tight in the stock, and the barrel is free-floated, then don't mess with it! However, bedding an action will not hurt anything (unless it is done incorrectly), so if it makes you feel better and gives you more confidence in your rifle, then it will be well worth the time and money.

On that note, whenever you see someone trying all sorts of *"remedies"* (because of reoccurring accuracy problems), things like trigger swapping, glass bedding, special process barrel cleaning, stock improvements, etc., the problem is almost always with other components, bad ammo, or the shooter. Many times, I have seen **pride** prevent a proper diagnosis because someone was too stubborn to examine the possibility that their reloads were faulty, or that they were simply flinching.

I myself had a batch of my own precision handloads that apparently got overheated in storage and led to unbelievable 18" groups at 300yds one day. I spent several days in denial of the possibility that it was bad ammo, and I was actually shopping for a new scope when someone *strongly urged me* to try different ammo. So, I unloaded the whole batch, reloaded the same cases and bullets with brand new powder and primers, went back to the range and proceeded to put the first 4 bullets in a 1-1/2" group at 300 yards! I was absolutely shocked! Now **I buy new powder and primers every time I reload**, and rework any ammo older than two hunting seasons.

14. **Quality components and a solid gun setup:** Do your research, talk to people, read articles, watch YouTube reviews and make your own logical determination about what caliber, rifle, and hardware you want. A quality barrel, a quality optic that will hold zero, and a solid mounting system for that optic are the three most important factors in any accurate rifle. Those three components mounted on a solid action are the core of every rifle. Rifle stocks are primarily there for your personal comfort, for looks, and to give you something to hold and attach a sling and bipod to. The stock should be sized to fit you and allow you to quickly acquire targets without having to stretch or strain your neck to get a good sight picture. Custom triggers and cheek plates are there to give the shooter better consistency. Go with components that make solid sense, like heavy or bull barrels and beefy one-piece scope bases and heavy rings... components that can take some real-world abuse and maintain shot accuracy. Some of the sturdier components may not be as attractive, so if esthetics is an important factor, build a rifle to take to the gun range that looks pretty, and then set up another rifle that you will actually take into the field and use to harvest animals at long distances.

My Walmart purchased, 100% factory, Remington Rifle

Most guys chuckle at me when I walk out to the 300 yard target and stick a business card on it, then walk back and lay down in the dirt with my hunting rifle. They always stop laughing after I put three consecutive shots on the business card… and they get really jerked when I tell them I bought the gun at Walmart! Though there is nothing wrong with buying a $6,000 hunting rifle, spending a fortune on a gun will not guarantee its accuracy… simple as that. Plan on spending at least $2,000 on a rifle, scope, base, rings, bipod, gun case, and range finder. Do your research, talk to other shooters, look at reviews online, and buy items that you feel good about for their functionality, durability, and quality.

15. **Leave emotion out of your equipment purchases:** The single biggest factor in emotional purchases is price point. Most people believe that they *must* spend an absurd amount of money in order to get the quality necessary for precision shooting. Don't just buy the *"most expensive"* stuff and expect it to be good… I can tell you there is a lot of really pricey hardware on the market today with all kinds of gimmicky claims that will leave you very disappointed. It is the job of every manufacturer to convince you that they have *"revolutionized"* some aspect of shooting sports, and that you must buy their product in order to be a great marksman/hunter… Don't buy into the hype!

    "Bragging rights" often plays into the purchase of new guns as well, and that is totally okay. We should all be proud of our guns and want to show them off… it's what we humans do when we are passionate about our toys. At some point during the purchasing process, we often have to make choices between guns that are *"cool"*, and guns that are *"practical and effective"*. Don't get so emotionally stuck on *"cool"* that you end up with a rifle or accessories that don't allow you to take down that once-in-a-lifetime trophy at 700 yards… Do you really want to be known as the guy with the *"Totally Awesome Rifle!"* that missed the shot at the *"Biggest Buck Ever"*?

    Oddly enough, there is also a sector of emotional sportsmen who are overly optimistic, and believe that incredible deals can be had on off-brand equipment that somehow has amazingly high quality... This is where the old adage, *"if it sounds too good to be true, it probably is"* comes in to play. Again, do your research, look at reviews online, and buy items that you feel good about because of their performance and functionality.

16. **Leave emotion out of cartridge choice:** The second biggest emotional factor in equipment purchases stems from articles and hype in magazines, claiming some new cartridge, with out-of-this-world ballistic capabilities. The reality is that there hasn't been a new cartridge developed in the past 40 years that *significantly* outperforms any previous cartridge in any area except for the exorbitant price tag… (**that ought to upset a few folks**). These new cartridges are typically the brainchild of someone trying to make a name for themselves in the shooting world, and they typically come with outlandish claims, that later prove to be *greatly exaggerated* after some independent field testing. I regularly see articles of new cartridges that shoot the exact same bullet, at the exact same speed of previous cartridges, yet *somehow,* they magically claim more foot pounds of energy and flatter trajectories. If you read about any new cartridge that claims more than about a 5% increase in any aspect of its ballistics, they are either comparing to really poor performing

cartridges, or.... you are not reading the truth. Typically, this 5% increase comes with a 30-50% increase in cost.

This is not to say that many of those new cartridges do not actually perform well, they simply don't perform *significantly better* so as to justify either the price or the lack of variety in available ammunition or reloading components. For instance, there are currently three times more available projectile options in 30 caliber than any other caliber, and in some calibers you will be lucky to have 10 choices in bullet type/weight... so why would you want to pay more money for less choices, and possibly having to settle on a less-than-optimal load for your rifle? *It may still be a 5% increase in performance however... and that's a good thing,* so you don't have to completely rule out all of the new cartridges.

Here is a list of some of the *"old standards"*... the *"tried and true"* cartridges... just to give you an idea of how long some great cartridges have been around. (Not all of these would be ideal for 500 yards and beyond):

Cartridge	Year Developed
30-06 Springfield	1906
270 Win	1923
300 Weatherby Mag	1944
308 Win	1952
243 Win	1955
223 Rem	1957
7mm-08 Rem	1958
338 Win Mag	1958
7mm Rem Mag	1962
300 Win Mag	1963
25-06 Rem	1969
338 Lapua Mag	1980

We all have our personal beliefs and biases regarding the best cartridges available, though I highly recommend simply picking up a current reloading manual, and browse through the muzzle velocities of different bullet weights for various cartridges BEFORE you go out and buy a new long-range rifle. You will start to see a pattern that shows the ideal weight-to-velocity ratio coupled with a high ballistic coefficient projectile to give good knock-down power and flat trajectory. Many of the *"old standards"* fall into this pattern nicely, and with the development of modern projectiles, these can be some very flat shooting rounds.

17. Plan on reloading your own or paying big $ for ammo: Ammo load quality and consistency is imperative for accuracy at longer distances. There are not a lot of precision reloading companies out there, and even fewer that cater to hunters and their ammunition needs. These manufacturers can charge upwards of $10 per round, while reloading the same at home may only cost only $1.50 per round. One way or another, if you have the commitment to become a long-range marksman/hunter, then you need to make precision ammunition a commitment as well. The difference between average off-the-shelf ammo and precision handloads can be a 30" group at 600 yards versus a 5" group… which is the difference between a miss or a clean kill. Reloading your own offers the ability to dial in the best powder load for your particular rifle and your specific choice of projectile. Buying the best off-the-shelf match grade ammunition may be a reasonably good solution, though it limits your bullet options.

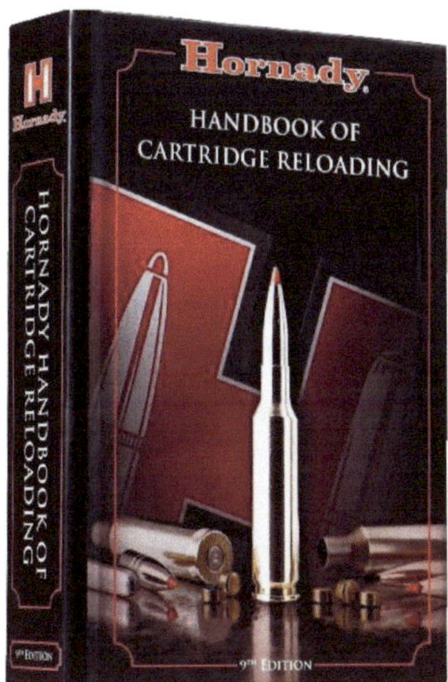

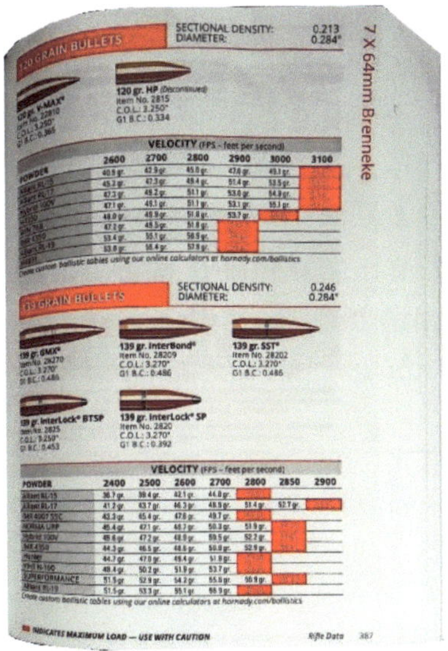
7 X 64mm Brenneke

SECTIONAL DENSITY: 0.213
DIAMETER: 0.284"

SECTIONAL DENSITY: 0.246
DIAMETER: 0.284"

A good reloading manual has a mountain of information to help you decide on a projectile, powder, or cartridge.

Bullet selection is the first place to start with reloading, and only polycarbonate tipped or solid copper tipped projectiles should be considered, as even the slightest nick in the tip of a soft point bullet can have huge effects on accuracy. Boat-tail bullets with their high ballistic coefficient (B.C.) are preferred because they simply cut through the air with less drag, and shoot flatter. The higher B.C. bullets carry better at distance, though there is the tradeoff in that they tend to be heavier as the B.C. increases, thus causing velocity (f.p.s.) to be lower, so you need to look at ballistics data for a lot of different bullet weight/f.p.s./B.C. combinations. Remember that heavier bullets carry farther with more impact energy at long distance, though a lighter bullet may shoot flatter.

An exaggerated example of this relationship is: A shot-put at 70 f.p.s. has as much energy as a BB at 6000 f.p.s., but neither one of those can kill a deer at 800 yards… the same is true with bullets, so you will probably settle for something in between super-heavy and super-fast. For *long-range* purposes, I highly recommend any cartridge/rifle combination that will send a 180-220 grain boat-tail bullet down range at 2800-3100 f.p.s. for any North American big game. Within those parameters, you will still have hundreds of bullet/caliber options to choose from.

One of the most misunderstood causes of ammunition related inaccuracy is *"too much"* or *"too little"* powder for your particular length of barrel and projectile. More powder may make your bullet go faster, though it may also lead to erratic powder burn, or destabilize the bullet as it exits the barrel causing poor flight characteristics and larger groups. Once you decide on a projectile, powder type and primer, you have to determine the optimal powder load for that bullet and your gun (this is where reading lots of reloading manual figures and talking to experienced reloaders and target shooters comes into play). This is done through 5 to 8 series of 5-round tests with ½ grain increase in powder loads per series to find which powder load will give you the best grouping. Example: 5 shots with 168 grains of powder then 5 shots with 168-1/2 grains of powder then 5 shots with 169 grains of powder… and so on until you find the tightest grouping. With a little luck, you will find this information from someone who has the same gun, caliber, bullet combination and has already proved the setup.

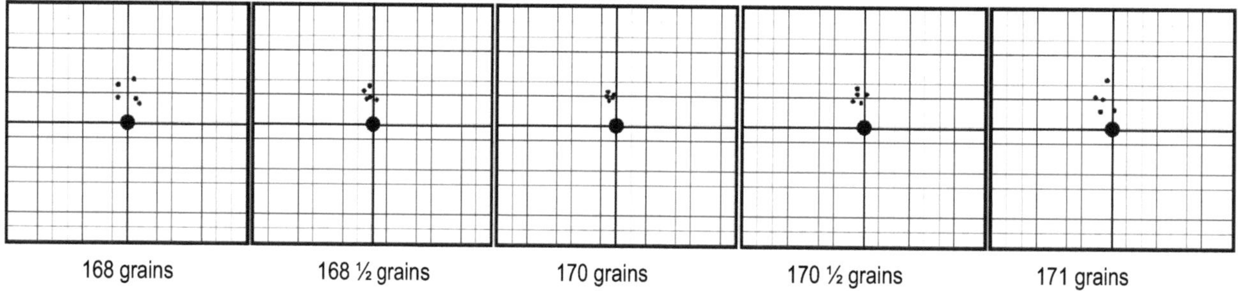

An example of five targets with powder load testing for grouping size.
This shows 170 grains powder is optimal for this cartridge/bullet/rifle combination.

Once you have everything from primer type, powder type, exact powder load, bullet type and weight, case measurements, sizing and crimp die settings, etc., and the gun is giving you sub-m.o.a. groups consistently…. DON'T CHANGE ANYTHING in your reloading procedure!!! You don't use those dies for reloading anything but ammo for that gun. You don't EVER change primers or powder or bullets and you use only that ammunition on ALL your big game and small game… because it is simply the most accurate setup that you will ever have and it works!

Remember, that this ammo is now *"tuned"* to your rifle and may not work well in most other guns of the same caliber. This *"tuning"* process is not something that off-the-shelf ammo can come close to.

You may very well find a brand/type/weight of off-the-shelf ammo that gives you decent performance, though you may have to buy 12 different boxes to find one that works well in your rifle, and then next year they will discontinue that particular load and you're back to square one. Learning to precision hand load your own is well worth the effort, though you will need to educate yourself… this is where a knowledgeable friend and the internet come in handy.

Precision reloading doesn't require a lot of equipment or space to get started and produce very-high-quality loads… education about how to properly use the tools is the key.

Another common argument in bullet selection is terminal performance, expansion, and weight retention. Some hunters are so concerned with putting *"big holes"* in animals or *"doing the most damage"* that they gloss over the idea that putting a finger sized hole through both lungs of any North American big game animal will dispatch that animal reasonably well.

Soft nose bullets may open up better on impact though typically are not as consistent during flight, and non-boat-tail bullets have a much lower B.C. which make them slow down more quickly and drop faster. Ultimately, hitting your animal in the vitals is far more important than whether the bullet does maximum damage… anyone who has chased a wounded animal for a mile will confirm this. Harvesting an animal should NOT be a competition of doing the most damage. This is a process of learning how to make accurate shots on specific vital organs to cleanly dispatch an animal with minimal waste… who really feels the need to destroy both front shoulders and ruin all that meat?

A few key things to remember when loading your own ammo:

a. **Buy new powder and primers regularly** or every time you reload a large batch, they are both very sensitive to temperature changes, humidity, and they do have a shelf life.
b. Cases already fired in your gun once will fit better the second time and produce better consistency.
c. Measure every powder charge with a very accurate scale.
d. Measure every case and finished cartridge length.
e. **Dedicate the dies to one load setup** only and don't change the settings once you have it dialed in. This gives you excellent repeatability year after year.
f. Keep ammo well labeled with ALL the data for that batch, and keep each new batch in a separate container with a date. NEVER mix old and new reloads!
g. Powder and primers will degrade under the effects of temperature swings the continued vibration of bouncing down a thousand miles of gravel roads. Unload (with a bullet puller) any ammo that has been traveling around for more than two hunting seasons, and reload the cases with **NEW primers and powder**.
h. Putting your ammo on the dash of your truck with the defrost on, can overheat and completely alter the burn rate of the powder, causing huge accuracy issues.
i. Store all your reloading supplies and loaded ammo in a cool dry place until you need it.
j. Above all… **Enjoy the reloading process** and imagine every bullet hitting exactly where you want it to, because you did it right.

18. Use a ballistics trajectory calculator BEFORE going to the field: There are several on-line calculators and phone apps that allow you to simply plug in different values and print out results. They come in very handy while trying to decide which bullet choice to use when it comes time to load your own ammo as well.

After deciding on a projectile and powder load, you will need to shoot your gun/ammo combination through a chronograph to know your exact bullet speed (f.p.s.), in order to use the calculator accurately… again, friends with these toys become useful. Become very familiar with your ammunition and plug variables into the calculator so you know how temperature, elevation, humidity, and angle up or down affect trajectory. You can also plug in wind values so you will be better at instinctively judging crosswind corrections when necessary. Run hundreds of scenarios, so you can get a real *feel* for your gun's performance in real world situations and can quickly, and instinctively, apply this knowledge in that important moment.

One of the most misunderstood aspects of hunting in steep terrain is that bullet-drop is greatly reduced when shooting at angles up or down. For shots under 500 yards, a reasonably good (yet over-simplified) solution to these variable angles is to "*shoot the horizontal distance*". Most rangefinders have a function that automatically gives the horizontal or *"true ballistic distance"*. Gravity basically only pulls downward on a bullet for the horizontal distance it travels, so a steeper angle equals less bullet-drop.

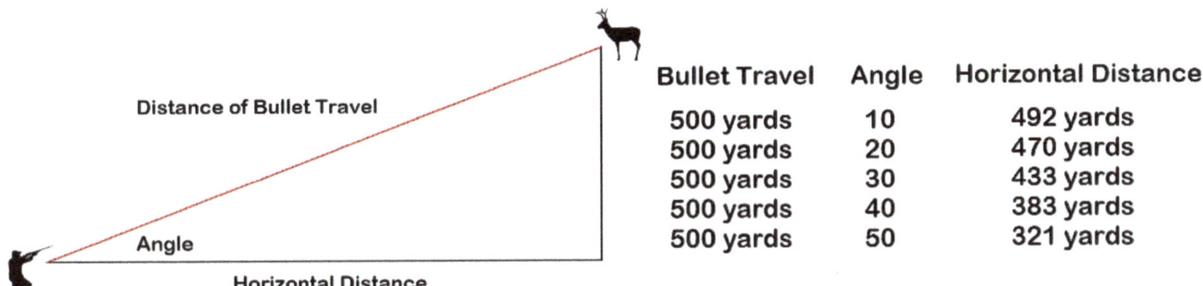

Bullet Travel	Angle	Horizontal Distance
500 yards	10	492 yards
500 yards	20	470 yards
500 yards	30	433 yards
500 yards	40	383 yards
500 yards	50	321 yards

Understanding the effects of angle on a shot is vital in steep terrain.

However, the amount of drag applied is determined by the distance the bullet travels through the air, and is directly affected by climate, density, and elevation factors. Shooting *the horizontal distance* is NOT a perfect solution. This is where having a ballistic reference showing how much less bullet-drop there will be at different angles can really help you make minor adjustments on the fly, without having to pull out a ballistics calculator. Some rangefinders have the ability to work with your specific ballistics, angle, temperature, and barometric pressure to give you a truly accurate elevation solution. These are awesome when they are set up and functioning correctly, though there is no substitute for *knowing* your ballistics intimately.

Having a full set of quick reference ballistics pages printed out for each hunt area is a must. The ballistics should be calculated for the hunt area/elevation, the average conditions for that time of year and multiples of temperature options in 15 degree increments. Print the pages in 50 or 25 yard increments, have multiple tables showing m.o.a. adjustments for different angles of elevation, and have the temperature and elevation highlighted. Reviewing this information will help you have a much greater instinctive ability in the field.

This being a *"practical"* guide, we are not going to get as technical as a military sniper school might be. There are many environmental factors that typically are not significant enough to make a substantial difference to bullet flight of 1000 yards or less. Rotation of the earth, a 10% humidity change, and a 0.05 change in barometric pressure are all things that a sniper shooting 2000 yards would be concerned with, however, a hunter taking a 700 yard shot at a deer would experience less than 1" of impact differential with these factors. It is possible to get *too technical* in your calculations, which ends up costing valuable time, creating additional distraction away from the target, and unnecessary frustration.

Learning to judge wind is an art that takes practice in the field and paying close attention to the grass, bushes, and trees in the moments before the shot. It is not uncommon for a 20-mph crosswind in your face to be a 10-mph crosswind in the opposite direction at the target. Always look at the wind effects on the surrounding environment at all distances between you and your target. Also remember that most animals like to be out of the wind as much as possible and will typically have almost no wind at their location no matter how much wind you are experiencing. A wind speed/direction indicator only tells you 25% of the true wind story of any shot and has been responsible for far too many poor shots at long distances. Shooting large 24"-36" targets at 300 yards (or farther) on windy days will really help you hone your understanding of how the wind affects your shot trajectory. Rely on your own instincts to figure the total effects of wind drift, especially in uneven terrain.

19. Simplify your ballistics calculation process: I have a set of laminated, waterproof, ballistic cards with different elevations and temperatures for my rifle/ammo, and I actually clear tape the appropriate card to the large end of my scope each time I go out. Some people have a clear holder on their forearm to put the ballistics card into. Having a completely hands-free reference allows me to hold my gun and a range finder without searching through pockets or having to use electronic devices.

Using these reference cards can save time over an electronic calculator, and/or offers a quick cross-check reference to ensure your electronic calculator is functioning properly. Always choose a card that matches the temperature and elevation for that day. It is also imperative that you zero your scope for similar weather conditions that you will be hunting in. Don't zero your rifle on an 80 degree July day and expect your zero to be the same on that 25 degree opening morning of hunting season. Ideally, it is best to shoot a test round at a 300 yard target to confirm zero whenever hunting in a new area, and I always do this to verify zero if my rifle takes a fall or a hard hit in the field.

Range	Flat	20Deg.	40Deg.
100	-3.5	-3.6	-4.0
200	-2.1	-2.4	-3.1
300	0.0	-0.4	-1.5
350	1.2	0.7	-0.7
400	2.5	1.9	0.3
450	3.8	3.1	1.3
500	5.2	4.4	2.3
550	6.6	5.8	3.4
600	8.1	7.2	4.6
650	9.7	8.7	5.8
700	11.4	10.3	7.1
750	13.1	11.9	8.4
800	14.9	13.6	9.8
850	16.7	15.4	11.2
900	18.7	17.2	12.7
950	20.7	19.1	14.3
1000	22.9	21.1	15.9

195gr 2850fps 4500' 35°

Range	Flat	20Deg.	40Deg.
100	-3.5	-3.6	-4.0
200	-2.1	-2.4	-3.2
300	0.0	-0.4	-1.6
350	1.2	0.7	-0.7
400	2.5	1.9	0.3
450	3.9	3.2	1.3
500	5.3	4.6	2.4
550	6.8	6.0	3.6
600	8.3	7.4	4.7
650	10.0	9.0	6.0
700	11.7	10.6	7.3
750	13.5	12.3	8.7
800	15.4	14.1	10.1
850	17.3	15.9	11.7
900	19.4	17.9	13.3
950	21.6	19.9	14.9
1000	23.9	22.0	16.7

195gr 2850fps 2600' 35°

These are two of the many laminated cards I have that I put on my scope.

All too often, the tendency is for someone to try to use a phone app or any number of specialized wind indicators with calculators, and more recently, devices that directly transfer hold-over to the scope with a lighted dot for the point of impact. These gadgets are fun to play with, can be very accurate at times, and do offer a great deal of insight as to the ballistics of your rifle while shooting at the range, but don't become so reliant on them that you can't make the shot in the field if something quits working. Electronic devices are subject to waterproof issues, difficulty reading the screens due to glare, dead batteries, cellular reception, and the little-known problem where 95% of electronic devices quit working at temperatures below about 15 degrees Fahrenheit. The latter is why I carry my range finder, phone, and camera in my inner jacket pockets when hunting in extreme cold conditions.

Too much reliance on gadgets can distract from the instincts that you should be developing naturally. I have witnessed hunters setting up a separate small tripod for their wind indicator/calculator, another for a spotting scope, and during this process of setup, button pushing, and shadowing the display so they could read it... the animal they were watching walked away... and to make matters worse, they didn't see which way the animal went! Afterward, they had to pack up all their goodies while the animal escaped to the unknown.

You should be able to quickly range a target, look at a basic ballistics table (perhaps taped to your scope or in the holder on your arm), adjust quickly for elevation, and then instinctively adjust your aiming point for slight temperature or elevation differences and possibly a crosswind... **You can do this!** because you have already studied a hundred different scenarios at home using the ballistics calculators *before* ever going into the field. Remember that your focus should be primarily on the desired target when the time comes, and every second that you are looking at a ballistics calculator, is another second closer to losing your opportunity at a trophy. Really *"get to know"* your rifle, ammo, and ballistics...Try to avoid getting "*gadget-dependency-syndrome*", especially in the field.

20. Your scope should be simple, powerful, and functional. Try to avoid reticles that are *too busy* with trees and hash-marks going every which way. They are quite often impractical, overly complicated, and extremely difficult read accurately in low those light situations when most animals are up and moving around.

A simple reticle with a few markings can be excellent for quick target acquisition and hold-over out to 400 yards, beyond that you will need to adjust the elevation knob to obtain truly accurate shot placement. At full magnification in most scopes, you will not have enough hash marks visible in the sight window to make a 600-700 yard shot without elevation adjustment, and the worst thing you could do would be to zoom out and try to count 15.7 m.o.a. and try to keep track of which mark (plus the .7) to put on the target.

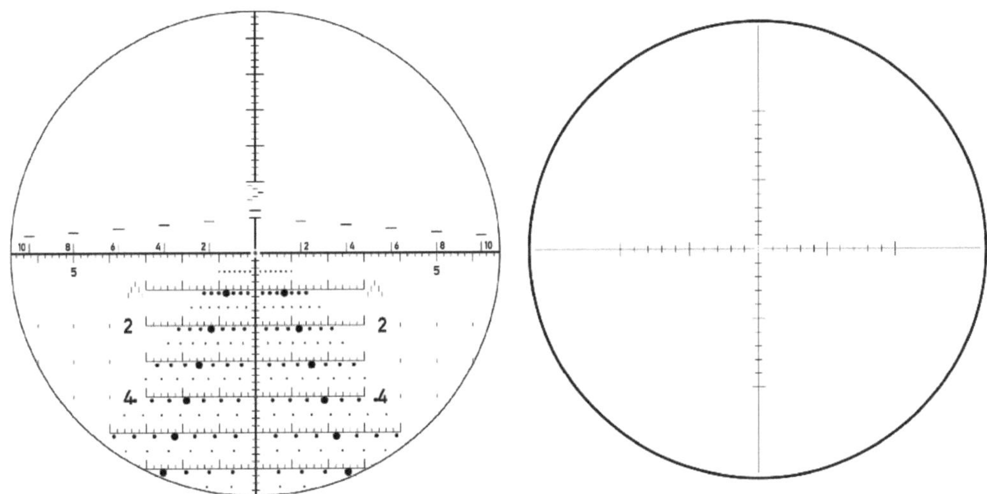

Find a scope with a "practical" reticle for hunting.

The reticle on the left is ridiculously busy and requires far too much mental focus away from the target… DO NOT use something like this for hunting! The reticle on the right offers simple m.o.a. marks, larger 5 m.o.a. hash marks for easy reference, and a clear sight picture… and most importantly, you don't need a PhD in math and physics to use it.

Most newer scopes have the side-focus, which is actually more than just an image focusing adjustment, it adjusts the parallax of the scope for particular distances. This is *very important to keep adjusted* to whatever range you are setting up for because it eliminates the movement of the crosshair on the target when your eye moves relative to the scope. If the focus is set for 300 yards and you are shooting at 700 yards, your shot could be off by as much as 24" if your eye is not perfectly centered in the scope… parallax is an important factor!

You will need a scope with at least an 18 power magnification, and I personally recommend 25 to 30 power so you can more accurately place your shot as well as judge the animal. If the crosshair paints two 12" wide stripes on the animal in your scope, DON'T take that shot! You need a scope that will allow you see that big 5 by 5 you spotted with your 10 power binoculars for the 2 by 3 that it really is… nothing is more frustrating than walking up on your *"trophy"*, only to be disappointed. I personally no longer *need* to carry a spotting scope while hiking because I have a scope on my rifle with enough magnification to properly judge a buck at 800 yards, though I do still carry good quality binoculars for quick spotting.

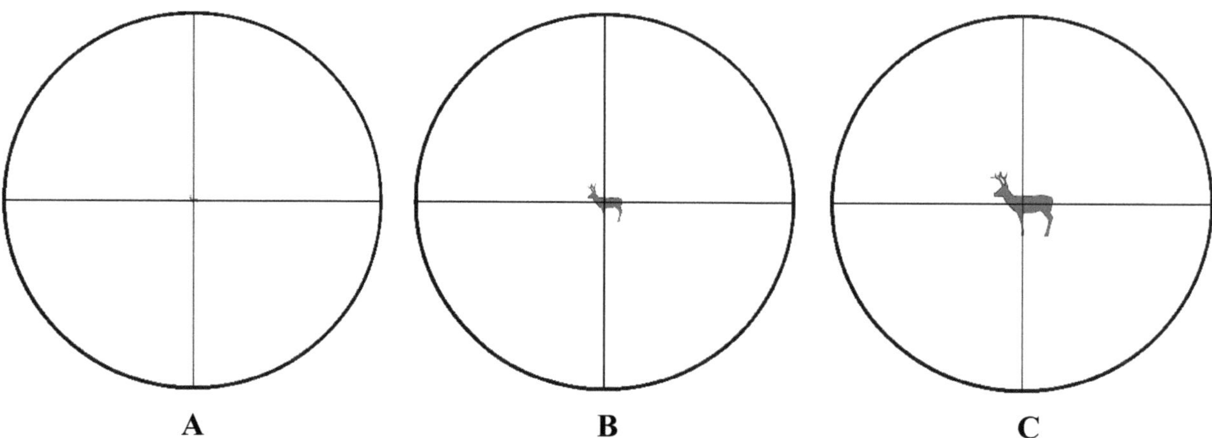

Image "A" represents 4 magnification at 850 yards… Completely useless! Image "B" is barely enough to make a shot, but without the ability to properly judge the target. Image "C" allows for very precision shot placement… and you can actually count the tines on the antlers. Make sure you have a scope that will allow you to have the benefits of image "C" (or better) out to 800-900 yards.

Purchase a scope with a large tube diameter and large objective lens to ensure good low-light gathering capabilities. As you look through the photos herein, you will notice many of the pictures were taken after dark. This is because many of my animals were harvested in the last 10 minutes of legal shooting light, well after the sun went down… that's when they come out to play. My 56mm objective lens gives significantly more light transmission than a 40mm or 50mm does, enough to actually see what I am shooting at during those *last-five-minutes* moments.

Lighted reticles can be helpful, and they can create problems as well. The most common issue is having the brightness set too high, causing the pupil in your eye to get smaller, which allows less light into your eye, and this makes the target image much darker and less clear, especially in low-light conditions. There can also be strange effects with the way your eyes and brain process the colors, partly due to the lack of color sensing cone cells in the peripheral areas of the back of the human eye… it often appears that there is only a partial image of the illuminated crosshair.

Using a scope with a single illuminated dot can cause a small halo effect, and result in difficulty placing the dot properly on the target. The illuminated *"dot-only"* in low-light conditions doesn't give you the *important* vertical reference line of the crosshair, and you may end up inadvertently tilting the gun, resulting in a shot being cast left or right as described in **#10**. Look through lots of scopes and read lots of reviews before deciding what will work best for you.

21. **Zero at 300 yards:** Remembering once again that this article is about *"Practical Long-Range Shooting"*, the single best thing you can do to make those long shots easier is to zero your scope/rifle at 300 yards. In any ballistic curve, the farther out the bullet gets on the curve, the faster it drops. By setting a zero point of impact at 300 yards, you effectively rotate the curve upward creating a situation where much less adjustment is needed in the elevation at greater distances.

    As an example, a zero at 100 yards that requires a 32 m.o.a. elevation adjustment at 800 yards may only require a 20 m.o.a. adjustment with a zero set at 300 yards on the same rifle. The same rifle may shoot 4" high at 150 yards with a zero at 300 yards, though it is very easy to compensate 4" down (with no scope adjustment) for a quick shot at a close target if the opportunity should arise. At the same time, with the zero at 300 yards, you can easily hold 3-4" high (again with no scope adjustment) if a target presents itself at 400 yards. Depending on your particular ballistics, you should be able to make any shot out to 400-450 yards with no scope adjustment or counting m.o.a. marks by simply setting your zero point of impact to 300 yards.

    "Rotating the curve" with a 300 yard zero makes a *huge difference* in the bullet drop-per-yard ratio from a 100 or 200 yard zero. With a zero set at 300 yards, the bullet drop between 800 yards and 825 yards may be 1.0 m.o.a. which is roughly 8" drop in 25 yards. The same rifle/ammo with a zero set at 100 yards may have a 16" drop in the same 25 yard window. Judging exact range and conditions becomes more critical as the distance increases and the downward angle of bullet descent increases, it is much more forgiving with a zero set at 300 yards.

    You will see the value of this information in the ballistics calculators/apps showing the variations between zeroing at 100, 200, and 300 yards and how that affects what you will need to do in the field in order to get shots on target.

22. **Most of all… Be proud of your accomplishments:** If you educate yourself, and practice what you have learned, you will be so very proud of the first time and every time you take a trophy animal at 600-plus yards with one shot through the vitals. It is no small feat, and those who truly apply themselves will be able to consistently and cleanly harvest animals at long distances in the field… it's worth every bit of time and effort.

What is a trophy animal worth to you?

When you start looking at the time and money involved with developing these skills, understand that the results equal the effort. A new bottle of powder, or a dedicated set of reloading dies, is a small price for a real trophy and the satisfaction of a well-placed shot. I put in a lot of time educating myself over 20 years so that if the day and time ever comes again where I have 15 minutes of shooting light and that 38" buck at 800 yards… I stand a 99% chance of looking at that rack on my living room wall before the next hunting season rolls around.

Cover Photo: 428 yard heart shot (animal bedded)

www.ingramcontent.com/pod-product-compliance
Ingram Content Group UK Ltd.
Pitfield, Milton Keynes, MK11 3LW, UK
UKHW060122300726
14090UKWH00002B/308

* 9 7 9 8 5 0 7 6 4 4 0 9 4 *